HOW TO HAVE **SEX** IN PUBLIC WITHOUT BEING NOTICED

MARCEL FEIGEL · ILLUSTRATIONS BY BRIAN HEATON

First published in Great Britain in 1983 by Frederick Muller
Frederick Muller in an imprint of Muller, Blond
& White Limited 55/57 Great Ormond Street,
London WC1N 3HZ

Reprinted 1983, 1984 (twice)

ISBN 0 584 11062 6

Printed in Great Britain by
R J Acford Ltd, Chichester, Sussex

COCKADE SEX SHOP